PLEASE RETURN TO

503/4 THE CHAMBERS

CHELSEA HARBOUR · LONDON SW10 0XF

TELEPHONE: 0171 - 344 1010

FAX 0171 - 352 7356 · 0171 - 351 1756

PETERS

FRASER

&

DUNLOP

Why do we have ?

DESERTS AND
RAINFORESTS

By Claire Llewellyn
Illustrated by Anthony Lewis

Heinemann

Contents

First published in Great Britain 1996
by Heinemann Children's Reference,
Halley Court, Jordan Hill, Oxford, OX2 8EJ,
a division of Reed Educational & Professional Publishing Ltd.

MADRID ATHENS PARIS
FLORENCE PORTSMOUTH NH CHICAGO
SAO PAULO SINGAPORE TOKYO
MELBOURNE AUCKLAND IBADAN
GABORONE JOHANNESBURG KAMPALA NAIROBI

Text copyright © Claire Llewellyn 1996
Illustrations © Anthony Lewis 1996

ISBN 0 431 06107 6 (hbk), 0 431 06109 2 (pbk)

A CIP catalogue record for this book is available at the British Library.

Editor: Andrew Farrow
Art Director: Cathy Tincknell

Printed and bound in Italy

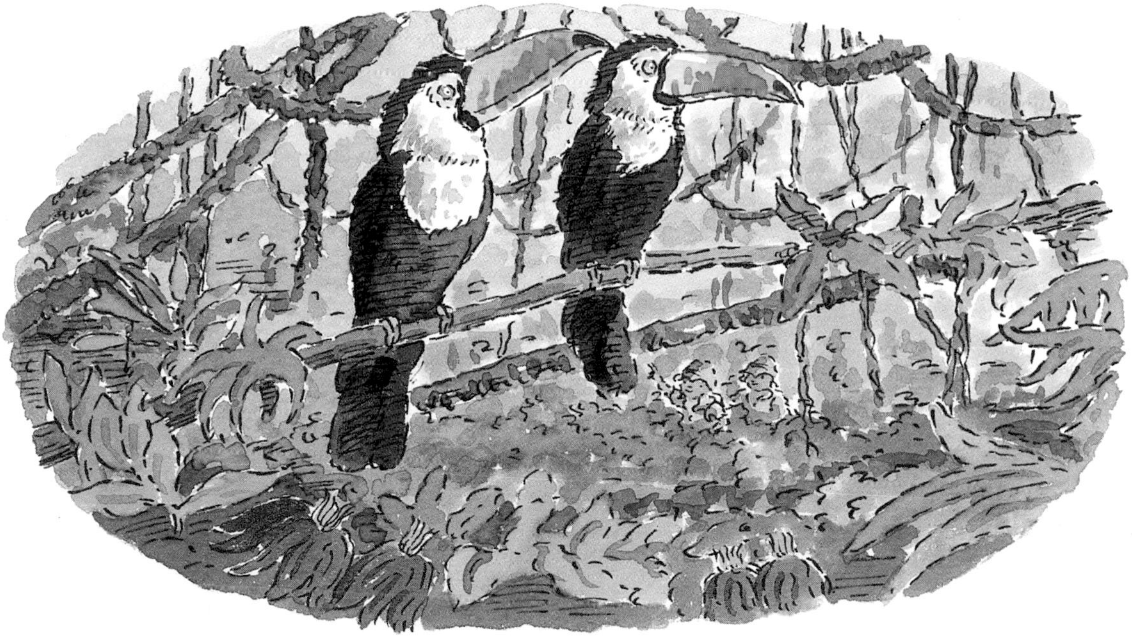

Wet or Dry?

Everywhere in the world has its own climate – a pattern of weather that is roughly the same year after year after year.

Deserts are hot and dry, rainforests are warm and wet. Why are they so different?

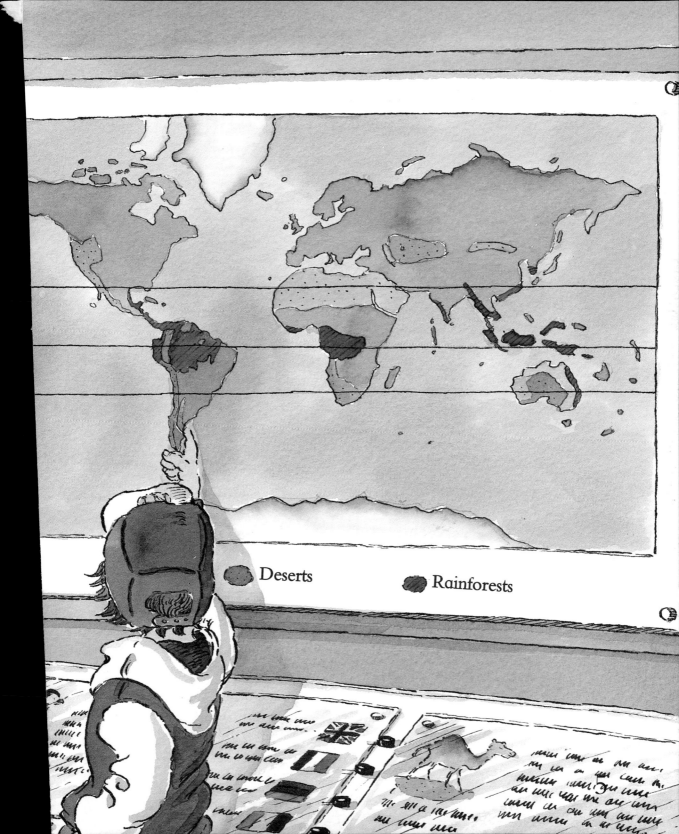

Deserts

Rainforests

Hot Days, Cold Nights

The world's winds carry water around the globe. The water makes clouds, which shower us with rain.

But the winds that blow across the deserts are dry. They are too dry to make a single cloud. Every day, the sun beats down from a clear blue sky.

Hot and cold

The hot sun bakes the desert

At night, the heat escapes

The skies are clear at night, too. When the sun has set, the warmth shoots up to the sky above, and the temperature sinks like a stone.

Growing in Sand

Deserts have no real soil. They are covered with sand, gravel or bare rock. These are difficult places for plants to grow.

Some plants have an extra-long root to suck up water from deep underground. Others store it in thick, juicy stems. All plants have leaves as tough as leather so the precious water can't escape.

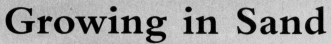

The wind blows sand into hills called dunes

Wind direction

Catching a Meal

Animals have a hard time in the desert. The days are too hot for hunting, so most of them rest under rocks or in cool burrows under the ground. At night they come out to search for food. Some animals chew prickly leaves and stems. But many are hunters, out to make a kill.

Living in the Desert

Some people have learned to live in the desert. Most are nomads, who move their goats from place to place in the search for food, water and grazing.

They find these at small water holes, called oases.

Underground water rises to form oases

After a few weeks, the food and water have all gone, and there is no more grazing. The nomads load up their camels and move on to the next oasis.

Recycled Rain

In just two weeks, a rainforest has more rain than some deserts have in a whole year.

Each day, heavy rain falls on the trees. The drops of water evaporate in the warm sunshine and rise high into the sky. Up there they cool and form new clouds. Then it rains once more on the forest below.

Trees take in some water through their roots

Growing Tall

Thousands of different plants grow in a rainforest. They thrive in the bright sun, warm air and heavy rain.

The trees are the tallest plants. They grow high to reach the sun's light, stretching out their branches to make a canopy over the forest. In the shade below them are lush ferns, creepers and big colourful flowers. Fungi and mosses grow on the damp forest floor.

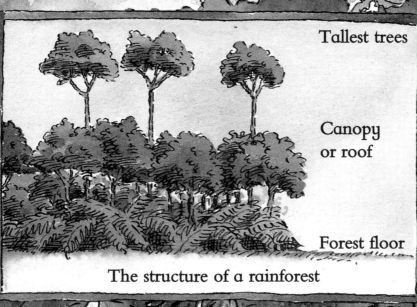

Tallest trees

Canopy or roof

Forest floor

The structure of a rainforest

Howl, Chirp and Shriek

Rainforests are noisy places, teeming with life. High in the branches, monkeys shriek and swing through the trees, while rainbow-coloured birds feed and call.

Lower down, frogs snap up flies, watchful for hungry lizards and snakes. On the ground, wild cats pace silently, as scurrying ants and beetles feed on rotting animals and plants.

19

Living in the Forest

People have lived in the rainforest for thousands of years. They live near rivers, in houses raised above the muddy ground. They move around on foot or by boat.

Everything they need, they find in the forest – food, fuel, building materials, and medicines that cure them when they are sick.

21

Protecting the Forest

Rainforests are under attack. People are cutting down trees for timber and to make room for mines, cattle farms and crops.

This is a disaster. Scientists have found treasure in the forests – plants that have given us foods, spices, rubber and life-saving medicines. We must protect the forests. Who knows what we will find in them in the future?

Destroying the rainforest

28

Index